NOT A
Cookbook

*A Confinement Project: My Almost 45 Years in the
Restaurant Business*

Marina Fiore

AuthorHouse™
1663 Liberty Drive
Bloomington, IN 47403
www.authorhouse.com
Phone: 833-262-8899

This book is printed on acid-free paper.

ISBN: 978-1-6655-1719-5 (sc)
ISBN: 978-1-6655-1718-8 (e)

Library of Congress Control Number: 2021903197

Print information available on the last page.

Published by AuthorHouse 03/01/2021

authorHOUSE®

Contents

*To all my regular customers and friends who
have supported us through thick and thin.*

Some since the very beginning.

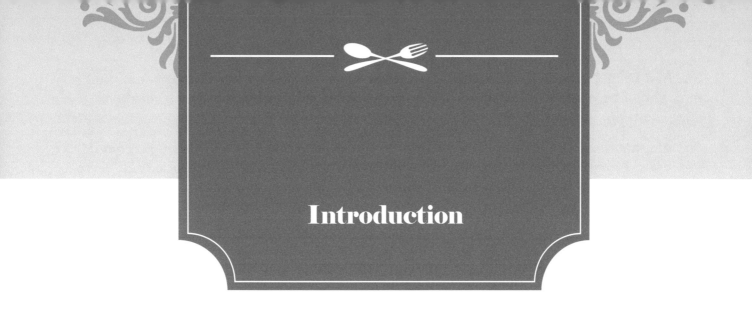

Introduction

This is not a cookbook.

I stole this introduction from Paul Gauguin's autobiography. He doesn't say, "This is not a cookbook," of course, but he says, "This is not a book."

And this is not a cookbook, either. It is a hodgepodge of memories – *lots* of memories. Some good and some sad. Mostly stories about my family and a few cooking tips.

And some recipes, too.

But, in reality, this is a Coronavirus confinement project.

Some recipes are not mine. They may be recipes of traditional dishes I love, recipes I borrowed from friends, many from my mother. But they all are recipes I have served and that some of you already had in our restaurant.

Many customers have asked me to write a cookbook over the years. My answer was always the same: when I retire. I have not retired yet, but this confinement is giving me plenty of free time. More than I'm accustomed to, really, and I need a new project.

Besides, something else prompted me to write this book.

Last summer, our first grandchild, Felix, was born and I decided to write and draw little books for him. In French, always in French. When my daughter heard I was already working on my 3rd book for him (on Coronavirus, no less!) she complained I had never written a book for her.

She had been the baby in our family for almost 30 years before Felix was born and had no intention of relinquishing her position. Thus, she asked me to write her one; a cookbook, she suggested. No, in fact she ordered.

So I did, and I enjoyed it so much I decided to write one for you as well. Although, I wouldn't put it past Anna-Caterina to have tricked me into writing this one by asking for one for herself. She knew I'd enjoy it.

So, I started writing the book you are about to read. Filled with memories, drawings, drawings of memories, cooking tips and drawings of cooking tips. Plus a few recipes.

I could fill pages and pages with memories. After 43 years of being a chef in the restaurant I have always owned with Patrick, my husband, what do you expect? A book with no memories? That would not be our restaurant and it certainly would not be us.

After more than four decades in this business, we are seeing the third generation in our dining-room: the grandchildren of customers who came when they were starting their life together – some as early as 1977 – when we were starting ours as well. Some of those people even had their first date here. Isn't it something?

I hope you will enjoy this book and will find it useful, but remember:

This is not a cookbook.

Patrick hanging our first sign (1978).

CHAPTER 1

All About Chicken and Sauces

Indeed, I have not revolutionized the cooking world. I am no Paul Bocuse. I haven't even made any great contribution to it. I am no Julia Child, either. But for all these years (and still counting) I have cooked to the best of my abilities and added my own touch to dishes created by others, *without* changing their character. I have eaten too many "*Choucroutes*" and "*Cassoulets*" which, when compared to the originals, shared only the names. Or "*Tiramisù*" that brought my morale down rather than up. I never wanted to risk changing a dish's spirit through imitation. But thinner sauces, as little salt as I could get away with, and always fresh herbs (the norm today, but we are talking about 1977 after all) was enough to make my dishes lighter and still true to the originals.

One thing our customers have always appreciated is the way I cook my chicken breasts. "Your chicken breasts are always so moist," they often say. "How do you cook them?" This is how I do it and this method will allow you to prepare your chicken ahead of time and keep it in the fridge up to four days. On the day of your dinner party, you will only have to worry about preparing the sauce.

It is not the most conventional way to start such a book, even a "not-a-cookbook" book, but it is the less exciting part, so let's get it over with:

4 Recipes of Sauces for Chicken

- Caramelized Garlic Sauce/*À l'Ail Caramelisé* – My recipe.
- Tarragon Sauce/*À l'Estragon*. Easily found now but still a novelty in 1977.

- Hazelnut Sauce/*Aux Noisettes* – My recipe, too.
- Sauce Poulette. In this recipe, if you replace the wine and broth with beer, you will pretty much get my beer sauce recipe, which was published in the 1982 *Bon Appétit Favorite Restaurant Recipes* book.

First, I must explain one thing: my way of preparing sauces is not conventional. But then again, this is not a conventional restaurant, either.

I am the chef, sous-chef, line cooks, and just about every other person usually working in a kitchen. Even on a busy night, I do it all! I am to food what a one-man band is to music.

Hence, I had to come up with my own creative solutions. The only way I can cook for some 30 people plus an occasional banquet in the next room is to prepare most of my sauces ahead of time and add the precooked chicken at the last minute, either in the oven or the stove top depending on the recipe.

First, how to cook a chicken breast LPC style.

Start by preparing a light vegetable broth. In a medium-sized pot, place:

- A couple of quarts of water
- 1 tbsp. of salt and a bit of pepper
- Fresh herbs such as rosemary, thyme, or a couple of laurel or sage leaves
- 1 carrot cut in a few large pieces
- 1 celery stalk also cut in large pieces
- 1 cup of white wine. Dry is always better but any decent white wine will do, really.
- 1 large onion in which you will have nailed a couple of whole cloves. In French, whole cloves are called *clous de girofle*, which literally translates to "clove nails," and I enjoy the image it conjures up. So, I always talk about nailing cloves. You must understand, I spend long hours working alone and musing about humorous situations. Many of which get immediately sketched.

Woman shopping for a clove hammer.

It seems like a lot of trouble just to cook chicken breasts but once cooled, this broth can be frozen and reused. Besides, it will provide you with the base of your sauce.

Bring your water with all the ingredients added to a boil. Let it simmer for at least one hour. The longer, the better. You can even let it reduce to 2/3 of its original volume, at which point you'll be ready to cook your chicken. While your broth is simmering, clean your chicken breast of any pieces of fat. Chicken breasts are usually sold already split in half: two halves = one breast. Count one half per person which will give you plenty of cooked meat. It will be easier and faster if you buy them already deboned.

I remember very clearly our first dinner customers and what they ordered: mushroom crêpes. It's not too difficult to remember, we only had two entrées! One with meat, one without. The meat entrée was supposed to be *Poulet Basquaise* (chicken sautéed in a sort of ratatouille), but it ended up being Beef Burgundy.

It's not that I thought my chicken would not be good enough. When I left it at night to cool off on the counter (my parents always told me I should not put anything too hot in the refrigerator), it tasted and looked delicious! But when I returned the next morning, the chicken, onions, green peppers, and my 85°F kitchen had done their work and made my dish look like a volcano about to erupt! Of course, I wanted to cry, but I had no time to waste! I will tell you one thing though: it is amazing how fast one learns when one is under pressure.

The only other dish I knew how to prepare fast enough was *Boeuf Bourguignon*. So, Boeuf Bourguignon it was, and I am quite sure it is not what our first customers ordered for they were both vegetarian. They were a delightful couple in their late twenties who used to come to the Tao a lot, where I worked for a year before opening my restaurant.

Working at the Tao was probably one of the most useful things I have ever done. Not only did I learn a lot, but it brought us many customers! Some of you might not have been born when the Tao was around – it was a vegetarian restaurant which belonged to an ashram. I was not a member of the ashram, but by the time I was hired the restaurant had become very successful and the ashram members were no longer enough to operate it at full capacity.

The ashram only prepared vegetarian dishes for its members and when the ones who craved meat found out I was opening a French restaurant, they all flocked to Le Petit Café to eat the steaks we soon started serving.

Looking back, I realize how stressful it was. Not the work – I never minded that – but having a restaurant and knowing so little about cooking. So much to learn. Never again would a day off feel quite as good as it did in those days, though!

Okay, where was I? Ah yes, the chicken! Once your broth is ready and still simmering, place your pieces of chicken in it, cover and let cook for no longer than 8 minutes if your half breasts are about 8 oz. If the size of your breasts differs, apply the rule of 1 minute per 1 oz. of meat (i.e., 6 oz. = 6 minutes). Count the time from the moment you place the breasts in the broth.

When the time is up, turn the heat off and keep the chicken in the pot for a couple of hours. It will keep on cooking in the hot broth and will remain moist.

It is a rather easy but long process, and you must organize yourself. For instance, you can prepare the broth and even cook the breasts the day before you need them. When the broth is a bit cooler put the whole thing in your fridge. The chicken will be ready the day of your dinner and you will only have to worry about preparing the sauce. If you keep your fridge nice and cold, cooked chicken breasts can remain stored in the broth for 3-4 days for sure. Besides, many herbs such as rosemary have preserving properties. As a matter of fact, a rosemary or sage plant would be very useful. You may even be able to keep them alive during the winter in the ground and covered with plastic. They grow quite large and can survive in cold temperatures.

You will also need to prepare a *beurre manié*. It's just soft butter mixed with an equal weight of flour (weight, *not* volume).

When preparing a sauce for my chicken, I prefer adding the flour at the end rather than the beginning. That's where the *beurre manié* comes in. For one pint of sauce – which is enough for four people – count one ounce of butter and one tbsp. of flour.

The best way to proceed in order to avoid lumps is to add a small amount of the warm sauce (like half a cup) to the *beurre manié* and whisk it in to loosen it up. Then you can add it to the rest of the sauce and put it back on a low heat. Whisk until it thickens and give it a quick boil, just a minute or two.

Random Le Petit tip (because a potato purée is always delicious with any chicken dish):

For a moister potato purée, add a pinch of baking soda to your potatoes before mixing with your other ingredients. It will aerate your purée.

Where is the sauce?

As I said, I always did the best I could, and we always tried to give our customers a good deal for their money. Over the years, we've always kept the same format that was the norm when we started: a soup or salad and two side dishes with each entrée. Most people have been happy to dine in our establishment, but one can't please everybody, right? I assume people who do not like us are not reading this book, anyway.

The following recipes are intended for about six people. It may seem like a lot of sauce, but sauces are what make French cuisine so unique. Well, I should say *used to* make our cuisine so unique. Whenever I go to France these days, I often feel disappointed to see just a thin thread of sauce surrounding the meat. Our regulars often joke, "Just bring us the sauce with plenty of bread!" Actually, they don't joke; my sauces are one of the reasons why people come back. And my husband insists on bringing a soup spoon with every entrée.

We shall start with one of the very first sauces I prepared for the restaurant and which is still one of our customers' favorites, especially the richer version.

Tarragon Sauce (Regular)

You'll need:
- A couple of nice shallots, minced
- Some fresh tarragon, at least 3-4 tbsps.
- 1 c. of white wine. For a stronger flavor, you can also use Marsala or Madeira wine instead of white wine. A bottle of dry Marsala would be a good thing to keep in your kitchen cabinet, anyway
- 1 c. of chicken broth (My way of cooking the chicken provides me with the broth I need for most sauces)
- ½ c. of cream. You may want a little more. Whenever I mention cream, I always mean whipping cream
- Beurre manié made with 1 tbsp. of flour and 1 oz. of butter

In a pan, sauté your minced shallots until they look tender. Add your tarragon and stir. Add your wine and broth, a little pepper and salt. Let it simmer, uncovered, until it reduces to 3/4 of its original volume.

Your sauce is now ready to be thickened. Add your beurre manié the way I explained earlier.

Add your cream, check the saltiness, and give it a quick boil.

This sauce, rather than its richer version, is the one I suggest if you intend to warm up your chicken in the oven with the sauce, with cheese on top. Some type of Swiss would be my favorite.

Tarragon Sauce (Richer)

Ingredients are the same, but you do not need the beurre manié and you will need more cream. At least ¾ c. instead of ½. You can adjust the amount when you add it at the end.

Proceed as in the first recipe but let the sauce reduce until you only have one cup left. Add your cream and let it thicken, always stirring. Adjust saltiness. Being more reduced, it will have picked up more saltiness thus use very little salt at the beginning.

This sauce has a richer flavor, one I would describe as more French. But it would not do to warm up your chicken in the oven in it with cheese, as you may with the other sauces.

Just warm up your sauce first very gently if you prepared it ahead of time, throw your chicken breasts in and let it simmer for a couple of minutes. And, naturally, you could proceed this way with the other sauces, too, if you do not care for cheese.

My Hazelnut Sauce

The initial way to proceed is always pretty much the same.

Shallots are a must.

For this sauce, you must have ½ c. of Marsala – no other wine will give you the same flavor. You also need some hazelnuts. A couple of large handfuls will be sufficient for four people.

Before or while your liquid (shallots, chicken broth, Marsala) is simmering and slowly reducing, prepare the hazelnuts. Place them in a 400°F oven and bake them until they become quite dark. Let them cool off and rub them between the palms of your hands. Most of the dry skin will fall off, some can stay. Grind 2/3 of them, not too fine, and keep 1/3 whole for garnish.

Add the ground ones to your broth whenever they're ready. They can cook in the broth for however long the broth still needs to cook, but they should cook in the broth for at least 10 minutes.

Then, continue as you would for the sauces above (i.e., beurre manié and cream). Sprinkle the whole nuts on top of the chicken when you serve.

Le Petit tips:

As you know, water and oil do not get along and can make a mess on your stove if you add wet veggies into a pan which contains oil. Try adding a pinch of salt into your pan before you add the oil. It will help.

I need chemists to explain this. I will ask Mallory and James, Sunday regulars/chemists, the next time I see them.

Butter cannot stand high temperatures. To prevent it from burning or getting too dark when you're cooking meat or veggies, add a touch of oil. The temperature of the butter will go up without burning it.

The restaurant in 1977 and now.

Sauce Poulette

Proceed in the same manner as for the regular Tarragon Sauce (minus the tarragon) and use white wine. When the liquid has reduced, add some raw sliced mushrooms. Let the mushrooms cook until tender and finish the sauce with your beurre manié and cream in the same manner.

The amount of cream you add is up to your personal taste, but keep in mind that the flavor of cream must never hide the other ingredients. In other words, when you try your sauce the first thing you taste must not be cream. Cream is there to complement a sauce, not to steal the show.

My Caramelized Garlic Sauce

Melt at least 2 or 3 oz. of butter in a saucepan on medium heat and throw in a handful of peeled garlic. Let the garlic brown. Add a large tbsp. of brown sugar and cook until it looks caramelized, in other words, brown and gooey.

Add 1 c. of broth and ½ c. of white wine. You've probably noticed you add less liquid; this sauce does not need to reduce as much for it will pick up the garlic flavor very fast. But it still needs to simmer, covered, for about 30 minutes to cook the alcohol.

Pour the sauce through a strainer but keep the liquid. Purée the garlic in a blender or food processor and then whisk it back into the hot liquid. The puréed garlic will give the sauce a little substance, but it will still need some beurre manié, albeit less than usual. About half the amount you need for the previous sauces.

Et de la crème, toujours de la crème. Cream, always cream! If you want recipes with no cream, you will probably regret the money you spent. Although, maybe not.

Another thing before we close the chicken chapter: if you happen to cook for some gluten-allergic friends, you can use some cornstarch or rice flour instead of beurre manié to thicken the sauce. Keep in mind 1 tbsp. of cornstarch = 2 tbsps. of flour. Dissolve the starch in a little cold water first, add it to the sauce and let boil for a couple minutes.

At this point, you are probably wondering when the chicken comes in, right?

I am writing these recipes in a way which will enable you to prepare both the chicken and the sauce ahead of time, which may be more compatible with your work schedule. The chicken will keep for a few days in the fridge and so will these sauces (which can also be frozen, by the way).

The day of your dinner party, all you have to do is slice the chicken breasts, pour the sauce over them, sprinkle your favorite cheese (Jarlsberg will go well with all of these sauces) and warm them up in the oven at 400°F for at least 20 minutes. If you're trying to avoid eating cheese you can still warm it up in the oven with plain breadcrumbs.

These sauces, mind you, are very versatile. The light Tarragon or Poulette (with beer or wine) sauces taste nice on pork chops, too, which you can prepare at the last minute. The richer Tarragon sauce would be perfect on veal cutlets as well.

One morning, I saw signs that someone had broken into the restaurant during the night. I was looking around to see if anything had been damaged or stolen when something in the trash can caught my attention. It was a whole onion quiche from which a large bite was missing! It was obvious the thief had opened the refrigerator, found the quiche, took a bite, did not find it to his/her taste, and threw it away in the trash bin. It was terribly vexing. And confusing. Was it a man or a woman? The evidence made it impossible to decide.

At first thought, most women would have warmed it up in the microwave right next to it. But then again, most men would not have looked for the trash bin. Yes, I know, I am being biased but keep in mind I am old. I shared my thoughts with the police officer who came to inspect the place, but to my surprise and disappointment, he did not seem impressed by my deductions.

Well, whether it was a man or a woman, the person obviously lacked good taste: my quiche was delicious, even cold.

Reduction + butter or cream = French taste.

Remember that taste Julia Child discovered when she added butter to her fish sauce? It can be summarized in the formula I've just shared with you.

For instance, there's nothing easier than preparing a cream sauce to dress fish or seafood (mussels, scallops, or shrimp). Cook your fish or seafood by stovetop or oven (depending on what you're preparing) with a little white wine. I sauté most seafood in a pan. No need to add wine to scallops for they will render enough juice to be used as a base.

Meanwhile, sauté a couple of minced shallots in a little olive oil.

When your fish or seafood is cooked, take it out of the pan, keep it warm and pour whatever juice it has rendered into the shallots (strain juice from mussels first for it could be sandy). Add enough white wine to get one cup of liquid. If you cooked some scallops you may already have enough liquid, but still add a little wine to give it more taste.

Add pepper and a little salt (not too much and none for mussels) and let reduce by half. When reduced, add the spice or herb of your choice. Saffron is always a safe bet with fish, but just a pinch; it goes a long way. Besides, it is rather expensive. Paprika goes well too. I personally love capers with most white fish. Or a couple of sage leaves, dill, or rosemary if you prefer herbs. If you want the sauce *à la Parisienne*, just add a few sliced mushrooms.

Add a good piece of butter to your sauce when it is reduced (the amount is up to you, but I wouldn't consider less than 1 oz. per person) and twirl it in with a fork until melted. If your fish has gotten too cold, just throw it back into the sauce and let it simmer for a minute.

Time Magazine, affirming my philosophy on butter.

CHAPTER 2

Rabbit, Crêpes, and a Few More Entrées

We were amongst the first ones – if not the first ones – to put rabbit on a plate in this town, at least in my time. Our original clientele was 50% university faculty and had eaten rabbit when travelling abroad, especially in France or Spain. Another quarter were people raised on farms and happy to be reminded of a dish often prepared by their mothers or grandmothers. And the others were willing to try it.

Well, most of them.

Lapin à la Moutarde

- A plump rabbit, which may be found in select supermarkets or farmers' markets
- A good amount of Dijon mustard., no less than 2 full tbsps.
- 1 c. white wine
- 4 oz. of butter and 1 c. cream
- Herbs. Dried is quite acceptable for this recipe. I suggest thyme or a couple of crushed bay leaves

Cut your rabbit in no less than 6 pieces: 2 forelegs, 2 hind legs, and cut the breast piece in half.

Coat your rabbit with the mustard, place it in a baking dish, add the wine and any mustard you have left.

Slice your 4 oz. of butter over it and bake at 400°F for at least 50 minutes, maybe 60 depending on the size of the rabbit. Flip the pieces of cooked meat to brown evenly on both sides, add your cream and bake for 10 more minutes. Check the inside of the meat with a fork; it should be white, like chicken should be when ready.

Sadly, rabbit has gotten quite expensive. Rabbit and organ meat. Back in the day you could not even *give* them away, but now they have gotten quite pricey. And since we want to keep our prices on the low side, we do not prepare it as often as we used to. Besides – and I am going to sound a bit snobbish now, sorry – once something has become a trend it's just not as much fun to do. I could write a long list of things no one else was doing in those days: most organ meats, rabbit, fresh mussels, balsamic vinegar, garage doors which open to the street, fresh pesto, etc.

I am very happy that people are more exposed to foreign flavors, and you can't find a better town than Bloomington for that, but it slightly rubs me the wrong way when people come in but do not stay because we do not have outdoor seating. We actually opened an amazing deck above the restaurant in 1995 but so many people complained because of a few flies or the wind or dim lighting that we got tired and closed it. Now I may see those very same people eating outside with some truck churning cement a few feet away!

Not that it matters, really. I am just saying when we are done with something, we are *done*. We have come up with a few ideas when people were not quite ready for them, tried them, gave them up but never brought them back later. It's just the way we are, a bit stubborn.

But what makes me a bit angry, though, is to have to pay almost as much for a beef tongue as for a steak. Back in the day, it was so much fun to serve all that for cheap. Beef heart, sweetbreads, kidneys, tripes, there wasn't an organ too internal for us to serve!

Anna also *demanded* my recipe for meatballs. Nothing here you don't already know – Americans eat more meatballs than the French and Italians put together. Nevertheless, I will write it here as a recipe you can also use to stuff peppers or tomatoes.

Stuffing for Peppers/Meatballs

- 1 lb. ground lamb or beef, not too lean. I suggest lamb for peppers, beef for tomatoes
- At least 4 to 6 garlic cloves, 1 onion
- 1 egg, salt, pepper, and your favorite herb or just lots of parsley

Mince the onion and garlic and add it to your meat. Add the other ingredients and mix well. You don't have to add breadcrumbs, but they will absorb the fat and your meatballs will be moister. A handful should be plenty.

Bake at 375°F for about 10-15 minutes depending on the size of your meatballs and the degree of doneness you want.

If you use the meat to stuff peppers: I personally prefer the red, orange, or yellow ones as opposed to the green ones because they keep better if you have leftovers or do not plan on using them right away. This should be enough for 5 or even 6 nice peppers.

Cut the top off, wash them inside, and stuff them. Put the hat back on and secure it to the pepper with a toothpick (which I never did for my Thursday Buffet for fear someone would not see it. Or maybe I did it once and learned my lesson?). Put them tight against one another in the pan so they stand up. Pour a little white wine over them and bake at 375°F for one hour. You could also cut the peppers in half before stuffing them, in which case you can sprinkle cheese on top. And they'll bake faster.

Crêpes

I have many crêpes memories. They are one of the first things Mom taught me how to make and they're also linked to another good memory: whenever Dad was out of town for work, Mom would often prepare crêpes for dinner. A mandatory bowl of soup and as many sweet crêpes as we could eat.

Years later I hosted a group of young pupils from my children's elementary school and taught them how to make crêpes. The mess wasn't even as bad as I had anticipated. They all thanked me by sending me a card in the shape of a crêpe.

I should clarify: I call them all *crêpes*, but depending on where you are in France, savory crêpes may be called *galettes*. I do not differentiate at my Window (my kitchen window which I open during the farmers' market) for I fear it could lead to too many confusions and explanations on a busy morning.

If they are meant to be sweet, I prepare the batter with white flour and call them crêpes, if they are meant to be savory, I use buckwheat flour and call them buckwheat crêpes. And by the way, Bloomington, I am sharing my recipe with you, but you'd better keep coming to the Window!

For about two dozen crêpes, you will need:
- 3 c. of flour, 3 tbsps. oil or melted butter, 3 eggs, 3 tbsps. sugar and a good pinch of salt.
- 4 c. of liquid; it can be all milk or half milk half water.

Mix all ingredients with only half the liquid. When the lumps are gone, mix in the rest of the liquid.

Warm up your nonstick pan on medium-high heat. To spread your melted butter: prick a fork into a thick chunk of potato, as my Mom taught me, and use that instead of a brush. You won't get any bristles in your crêpes. When your butter sizzles it is time to add a small ladle of batter (about 3 oz.) as quickly as you can as you rotate the pan so the batter spreads all over. Let it cook until the top looks dry and the sides curl up. Flip it. You can use a large plastic spatula or throw it in the air if you feel confident (or do not mind a little extra clean-up). I use my fingers but don't if yours are not immune to heat like mine.

The other day I found an old TV cooking show from the early 50s, the only cooking show back then on French TV. Chef Raymond Oliver, whom I adored and watched religiously every Thursday afternoon, was making crêpes. I remember thinking if I sold those crêpes at the Window, I could get in trouble. The pint of milk is replaced by equal amounts of milk, rum, and beer! Plus, what looked like half a cup of vanilla, 8 eggs, and 3 or 4 times the amount of butter I use. It made me feel very cheap. If too thick, he said, add more beer.

Of course, I had to try it. Right away, too. And you know what? It was delicious!.

Buckwheat Crêpes or Galettes

Same as above but you use buckwheat flour instead of white flour and skip the sugar. No Gluten here.

For galettes you will need one more cup of liquid. You may have to add an extra ½ cup of water before you start making the galettes, for this batter thickens much faster, especially if you let it sit in the fridge for a while before you use it. You do not want it to be as thick as pancake batter, but it should not be as thin as sweet crêpe batter either.

If you like the taste of beer, this batter is delicious made with a light beer. No water then, just beer. If you prefer dark beer cut it with a bit of water.

Whether you prepare crêpes or galettes, you need to keep them warm. Just place them on a plate over gently simmering water.

Gâteau de Crêpes (savory cake of buckwheat crêpes)

Crêpes or galettes usually get eaten right away, but if you have some left, this is a good way to give them a second delicious (and gluten-free) life. You will need to prepare a GF bechamel. Nothing easier: dilute 1 tbsp. of rice flour into a bit of cold water and add it to one pint of hot milk. Turn heat down and keep on whisking until thick.

In a round baking dish just alternate the crêpes with a thin layer of GF Béchamel to which you have added your favorite cooked vegetable (mushrooms, spinach, leeks, etc.). Sprinkle some cheese every other crêpe, and top off with a crêpe, more cheese, and a bit of butter.

Bake at 350°F for about 30 minutes.

My mother during her last summer in
2008 at age 88. Always so elegant.

Pâte à Pizza de Mamy

My mother was Mamy to her grandchildren and I am continuing the tradition. She didn't often make pizza but when she did her crust was between a Focaccia and a Brioche.

And naturally I never wrote the recipe down. I would say 3 c. of flour mixed with a tbsp. of sugar and ½ tbsp. of salt. Half a cup of olive oil, 1 egg, about 1½ c. of warm milk. And yeast. I can't help you here, sorry; I always use the professional yeast, SAFR-Instant ®, which one can add directly to the flour. It's probably not available in supermarkets but one can usually find it at the local co-op. Or order it online. Terribly convenient. It comes in a 1 lb. vacuum-sealed package, but well-protected in a glass jar it will keep forever in the fridge. If you prefer using the conventional yeast, prepare the dough ball the French call *pâton* using yeast, a bit of flour and water. The way to proceed comes with any bread recipe.

Work the flour/sugar/salt into the pâton or just add 1 oz. of SAFR Instant® yeast. Quickly add 1 c. of warm milk (make sure it's not too hot, your finger should stand the temperature), the olive oil and the egg. Start kneading until it forms a smooth ball, about 10 minutes by hand or 5 if you have a blender with a kneading attachment. You may have to add more milk, and if you accidentally add too much, just throw in an extra handful of flour.

Put it in an oily bowl, cover with a towel and place it in a warm and dry place. If your kitchen is as cold as mine, warm up the oven a bit and turn it off. When just warm enough, place the bowl in it. Or wrap the bowl in a large towel away from drafts; over the pilot light is always a good spot if you have a gas stove. When its volume has doubled, punch it, roll it very thin and dress your pizza. Strangely enough, I do remember the pizza's baking time: 25 minutes at 425°F.

CHAPTER 3

Mayonnaise, Appetizers and Soups

Mayonnaise Maison

I usually use peanut oil mixed with ¼ of its volume of olive oil. Just olive oil by itself makes a mayonnaise which is often too strong to go with more subtle flavors, such as spinach for example. The only mayonnaise for which I only use olive oil is aioli, the mayonnaise of Marseilles. Speaking of olive oil, I'm reminded of something very funny the owner of a restaurant in Milan said.

Anna and I were touring northern Italy and, while in Milan, we spotted a quaint little place to have dinner. Come to think of it, most restaurants in Italy are "quaint little places." Being famished (traveling with Anna is like running a marathon with, thankfully, quite a few stops for food), we asked for two plates so we could dip our bread in that very nice olive oil on the table.

- "Ah!" exclaimed the owner. "You are American! I thought you were French."

Surprised (and slightly worried? American tourists still have the reputation of being loud), we asked why, and he told us asking for plates for the olive oil gave us away.

- "Only Americans do that," he explained.

I had stayed away from Italy for too long and had forgotten that in restaurants the olive oil on the tables is for the salads.

But, back to my mayo.

- 1 c. oil, 2 yolks

- A touch of mustard (which is not often mentioned in recipes but does help speed the emulsion process, especially if you whisk your mayonnaise by hand instead of using a food processor)
- A few drops of lemon juice or vinegar (use lemon if you need it for fish or for dressing a cold salmon; the lemon will give it a shiny color)
- A pinch of salt, unless you prepare a mayonnaise in which you plan to add salty condiments such as capers, curry, or pickles. Taste it before you add your salt

Mix all the ingredients but the oil. I assume you will be using a food processor or an electric beater.

Then, add the oil *slowly* so it has time to adhere to the eggs.

Doing it by hand with a whisk is trickier and much longer. First, find a whisk with as many wires as possible, the more wires the faster. Then you must respect a certain protocol: your ingredients must be at the same temperature which means you must take the eggs out of the fridge at least half an hour before you start, and you must add the oil very slowly. Mayonnaise is an interesting chemistry project: you know oil and water (represented here by the yolks) do not mix, therefore you break the oil in teeny, little particles before it can adhere to the eggs.

Do it by hand once, just to see if you can (it could impress your foodie friends!), and then use your food processor or electric beater. After we acquired our first Cuisinart® (the first food processor on the American market), I never went back.

Once your mayonnaise is ready, use it plain and add the condiments of your choice.

Mayonnaise is a Mother sauce and can give birth to many delicious new ones. *Sauce verte* if you add cooked spinach. *Tartare*, with shallots and pickles. If you add tuna, capers, and more lemon juice, you have the sauce for *Veal Tonnato* (the veal can be replaced with chicken or turkey). And the wonderful aioli I mentioned earlier, in which you throw a handful of minced garlic.

Allow yourself to be creative: serve your next shrimp with a choice of 3 mayonnaises; now those foodie friends of yours will truly be impressed! Aioli, curry and spinach for instance; 3 different flavors which complement one another very well.

My son loved a mayonnaise I prepared with fresh mango to go with lobster tails. With grapefruit is often done in France for shrimp to be served as an appetizer, in which case you would serve the shrimp in the grapefruit halves. As my husband says, the possibilities are endless.

Le Petit tip:

Do you want your spinach to keep its bright color when you cook it? Understandable.
Try cooling it in sparkling water. The chlorophyll (pigment which gives color) will stay.

On Appetizers

This won't take long; this is a book of most of our customers' favorite recipes and two of those are cheese pastries and escargots. The third one is my *Pâté Maison*, but I am not quite ready to part with that recipe. Sorry. When I retire, for sure.

Pastries are a no brainer: Phyllo + your favorite cheese + butter. The only thing you may not guess is that we use twice as much butter as you could imagine. It's the butter which makes those pastries fluff up when they bake. The magic of the butter.

Open your phyllo, brush plenty of melted butter, fold the long side in half. Place your chunk of cheese (about 1 oz.) one inch from the bottom, roll it up two-thirds of the way, brush plenty more butter, fold the sides over and finish rolling. Don't roll it too tight, leave a little room for the butter and cheese to breathe. And guess what? More butter on top, *bien sûr*!

Bake at 400°F until slightly brown and fluffy, about 15-20 minutes.

Escargots

Buy a can with shells, mix your soft butter with plenty of minced garlic and parsley. Add salt and pepper. Make your butter a bit salty for snails are very bland.

Put a little butter first so the snail will be stuck between two layers of butter (Anna thought of it all by herself!), then the little beast and finally more butter.

Bake at 400°F until the butter bubbles.

One thing recipes may not tell you is to let your snails soak for a few hours, even overnight, in red wine you have simmered for about 30 minutes with a few herbs like thyme and a bay leaf. You could add a little salt to that, too. They will pick up a little more taste because, like I said, canned escargots are rather tasteless. Unless you want to use the fresh escargots you see coming out after the rain? Those will be better, but it is a gross process I don't even want to describe in my pretty book.

Pâtés

Pâtes are popular and over the years I have tried just about every pâté I could think of: duck, rabbit, *Rillettes* with chicken, *Pâté en Croûte* or *de Campagne*. All delicious, but everybody's favorite is the *Pâté de foies de volailles*, the chicken liver pâté. I often prepare mine with walnuts or pistachios. Ironically, it is the least French of all my pâtés.

As I said, I should include its recipe here. Again, sorry. Maybe during the next confinement? I should not joke about this – not funny. I started this book at the beginning of the first wave and, as I am doing this first editing, we are in the middle of the second one.

I wrote a funny little book about Coronavirus for Felix, my grandson. I wrote it right at the beginning of the pandemic but, quite frankly, I do not think I would have the heart to make it so funny now. I'd probably make him cry, poor Felix.

Book on Coronavirus for Felix.

Do some of you remember the blizzard of 1978? It was our first confinement, and a very romantic one! Those few days snowed in while the blizzard made our house creak and all there was to eat was a box of cereal and a few canned apples were wonderful. It was so much fun, really, in a slightly worrisome way ("How long will it last?"), which made it even better.

Those were our first months in business when an average working day started at 8 a.m. and ended at 11 p.m. with (if lucky) only an hour between both shifts. Those few days of forced rest stuck in the house were a wonderful vacation.

In those days we lived in a beautiful farmhouse practically downtown. Incidentally, a few years later our house was used by Peter Yates for his Bloomingtonian film, *Breaking Away*. The crew would come just about every night to eat at the Café and we were asked if we knew of an old house available for a scene. It was a great deal for us: they paid rent while filming, trashed the house but repainted it and it looked ten times better than before! It was used in the scene when Jackie Earle Hailey lifts weights while his girlfriend visits and tells him about her new job.

I got to meet pretty much everyone involved in the filming or acting and I must say Yates was one of the nicest guys I've ever met. Roy Schneider was married to the film editor and I still remember he had a veal chop. I forgot what Dennis Christopher, Dennis Quaid, Daniel Stern, Paul Dooley and Barbara Barrie ate – although I do remember one of them was vegetarian – but I remember where they sat in what is now our lobby.

There is one very sad ending to this story: the missed beginning of what would have been, doubtlessly, my fantastic career in the film industry...

Peter Yates thought I would be ideal for the part of the French student at the very end of the film but left the final decision up to the art director to make. Well, sadly, she thought I was too old...TOO OLD?!? Surely a little make-up would have corrected that, don't you think?

This past weekend should have been IU's Graduation weekend here in Bloomington. Back-to-back with Mother's Day, too. Coronavirus changed all of that. Not that I have the right to complain; I have been ranting about Graduation weekend for the past 20 years and some of you may think I finally got what I wanted. Not exactly.

I missed the income, which carries us during a part of the slow summer. I missed the people who were planning to celebrate with us, and I also missed the hard work. Working very hard when things are well planned is a lot of fun.

What I did not miss, though, were the people who would reserve and not show up – not even a phone call to cancel. After inquiring on two separate occasions about vegetarian options, the possibility of bringing a last-minute guest or their own Champagne, there was no time to place a third phone call?

My philosophical son usually reminds me some people don't even know we are a *Maman et Papa* restaurant. True, but this particular Maman takes it personally. It's actually a miracle I haven't had an ulcer yet. I guess I wasn't meant to have one. Or maybe it's the red wine which washes it away before it has time to settle.

But personal sensitivities aside, it saddens me to see people graduating and having learned so little about decent human behavior. Not to mention these same people are now ready to enter the workforce, some in politics or financial institutions. That, my friends, is frankly worrisome.

But this is neither a cookbook nor an essay on our modern society.

Patrick and me in the dining room.
Courtesy of Jennifer Weiss

In this "not-a-cookbook" of a few recipes and memories, I only allowed myself to rant twice. Not bad at all for someone who has been in this business – not for 20 or 30 years – but for 43!

A restaurant owner who writes a book and who doesn't have one thing to complain about is the stuff of fairy tales. Even in the nicest places owned by the nicest people who only hire the nicest help and are supported by the nicest customers (yes, like us), there will be occasional complaints in the back, the kitchen, or the waiter station.

Sadly, sometimes about the kindest client, unaware of the level of stress on an unexpectedly busy evening, who asked for more water at the wrong time. Nothing personal, it's just human nature. Frustrations have to be vented, that's all. Fortunately for you, Patrick, to avoid such unpleasantness, had the good idea to bring a pitcher of water to each table.

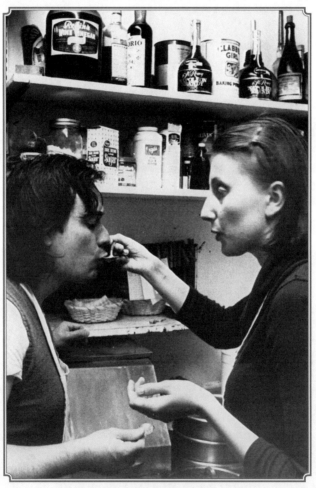

Patrick tasting the soup 1977.

About Soups

When I told my friend, Maureen, I was writing a cookbook (kind of), she asked me if it was going to be a real cookbook with sections for appetizers, soups, etc. It's not exactly that – actually, not at all – but now I feel like I should include a couple of soups.

I never buy vegetables for soups; my soups are about what I have in the cooler or the pantry and there is always what I need to make a soup. Unless I need 20 lbs. of leeks or something like that.

Carrot Soup with Cumin

Sauté some shallots (the French are fond of their shallots. I remember before shallots were a thing here, we could only find the ones imported from France and they cost a fortune) and add your 2 lbs. of carrots, peeled and coarsely cut; they will get pureed anyway.

Add enough water to cover the top, add salt and pepper. Plus, some cumin. Up to your taste but I would not put more than 1 tsp. to start. Let the carrots cook, purée them, check your salt and cumin, and the consistency of it. If you find your soups are too thin, you can always add a tbsp. of rice flour diluted in a bit of water and let it simmer for a couple of minutes. If too thick, a little water will do.

Serve it with cream. If you want to make it fancier, add an egg yolk to your cream.

My cauliflower soup follows pretty much the same method, but I add milk instead of water and one handful of rice at the beginning. My favorite spice for this soup is nutmeg.

> Le Petit tip:
>
> If you want your cauliflowers to remain white, add 1 nice tablespoon of flour to your cooking water.

The restaurant dining rooms.

One of my favorite stories to share about our restaurant is that it has been part of so many couples' happiest memories: first date, wedding, dinner to celebrate a baby on the way, or a wedding anniversary.

Unfortunately, our café sometimes becomes part of their saddest memories, too. It has happened before that I approached a couple to inquire about their meal and was met by silence and eyes filled with tears. I am so sorry, my friends. I wish I could bring your lost love back but all I can do is bring you more bread or a little more sauce…

I then realize it is all going to change for us. Yesterday we were their favorite restaurant to celebrate the romantic events of their life, and now we are the restaurant where they decided to get a divorce. It happens that I'll see one of them months or years later in a store. "So sorry," they usually say, "I have not been back in so long. I will come back soon!"

I know they won't. Why should they? Within a few days our café was demoted from a happy place to a sad one. They seem happy again, though, but they are now happy with another companion in another restaurant.

There is one African soup I particularly like: a lentil soup made with a couple of sliced bananas. I haven't made it in a while, but I probably added more exotic spices to it such as cumin, a little cinnamon, a touch of cloves and – since I like it a bit spicy – just a touch of cayenne pepper.

Cook the lentils (you do know lentils are the only legumes which do not require soaking, right?) in plenty of water with the spices. The ratio is about one quart per cup of lentils. Purée about half of the lentils when they are done and stir them back into the pot. Serve it with yogurt. Excellent cold, too.

As you can see, I like simple soups. I stay away from soups that involve two dozen different ingredients. Not that I do not enjoy them; maybe I'm just lazy. Unless I make a Minestrone which, strangely enough considering I am Italian, I seldom do.

When I blend a soup, I always leave a small portion of it chunky. It's just a habit of mine. Maybe it just started at the beginning when I wanted to make sure our customers would know I made the soups from scratch? Who knows?

When preparing a soup meant to be served chunky, Mom told me to throw a couple of peeled potatoes in it, fish them out when done, purée them and pour them back into the soup. It gives it a slightly thicker background.

I just remembered her pumpkin soup, the way it is prepared in Piedmont (Northern Italy) or maybe just in Turin? You clean, peel, and slice your pumpkin in big chunks and prepare the soup the same way you'd make a cauliflower soup. With shallots, milk, rice and nutmeg. Not my most popular soup but I love it. In this case blend it all, no chunks.

She also taught me a funny trick: when preparing an onion soup, cut an onion in half, burn the two sliced sides in a bit of butter and throw them into your soup while it's cooking. It will give a darker color to your broth. I recommend it if you make a vegetarian onion soup which tends to be pale in color.

Le Petit tip:

Tired of crying a river when you peel onions? Put the onions in the freezer for 10 minutes or in the fridge in a bowl of cold water for 30 minutes. Onions do not like the cold and will not release their gas.

Me, preparing my strawberry soup.
Courtesy of Maria Vettese.

I can't believe I almost forgot my famous strawberry soup!

- 1 lb. of strawberries
- 1 pint of red wine
- 1 or 2 tbsps. sugar, spices.
- Cream. Always.

Put your quart of clean strawberries in a pot and add just enough red wine to cover them (you can do half wine and half water, but no less wine than water) plus 1 to 2 tbsps. sugar, depending on the sweetness of the berries. Add a good pinch of cinnamon, too, and maybe a hint of cloves.

Cook for about half an hour.

Strain the fruit (keep the wine, of course) and put it in a blender. Add some of the cooked wine to it plus 1 tbsp. of cornstarch that you have mixed with a bit of water first.

Blend well until smooth. Pour it back into the pot with the rest of the liquid and back on the stove. Cook gently while stirring until it has thickened a bit. Once cold, add the amount of cream you desire.

This will give you a good quart of soup, enough for 4 to 6 people.

I studied art for a couple of years, then did temp work for one more until I decided to follow my then boyfriend, Patrick, to the United States where he was studying percussion at IU. For three years, I waited tables in various Bloomingtonian restaurants until we opened our own. Until the early eighties, my parents had no idea what direction my life would take next.

I've often imagined the many conversations about me my mom had on the telephone with the same aunt I am about to call:

- "Is Marina doing well in school?" my aunt – my *zia* – would ask.
- "She was...but she quit," my mother would respond. "Oh, just for a while! She wanted to take a break and work for a bit."

- "Oh…"

Later.

- "Is Marina enjoying working?"

- "She was…but she quit. She is going to America with Patrick."

- "Ah…?"

Later.

- "Is Marina happy in America? What is she doing there?"

- "She is working in a pizzeria."

- "Pizzeria?!" (Not saying it but surely thinking I could have done that in Paris.)

Later.

- "Is Marina still working at the pizzeria?"

- "No, she works in a restaurant on a beautiful lake." (Then a steakhouse and a vegetarian restaurant…)

Later.

- "Is Marina still in that vegetarian restaurant?" (Keep in mind that 40 years ago, the mere concept of a vegetarian restaurant was not an easy one to grasp for an older Italian person.)

- "Actually, Marina and Patrick are going to open their own restaurant."

- "………"

- "Dear? Are you there?"

- "Si, si! Sorry!" (Zia had most likely dropped her cup of coffee on her lap and was silently enduring the pain.) "Did you say they were going to open a restaurant in America?"

- "Si. But I do not think it is going to be vegetarian."

My parents have been long gone but it still brings me comfort to know that for some 30 years they were proud to tell their friends and relatives I was doing well. That I had found my calling and was happy.

Confinement Thoughts

Confinement hasn't been too difficult for Patrick and me. Well, apart from nearly no money coming in but bills still punctually arriving.

I have kept busy on my books for Felix, and now this one for you. And Patrick has been taking advantage of this forced parenthesis to tile the big kitchen.

In the evening we watch movies or old series on Netflix. We're always a few years behind because we do not have cable. Lately we have been watching *Dexter* and *Six Feet Under*, the former taking place in Miami and the latter in LA.

If you know our building, you have noticed my husband is a stickler for simple geometry, symmetry (very important), and proper alignment. In this case, of tiles.

Our confinement would be idyllic (we have always been together 24/7, therefore there's no getting-used-to tension here) if it weren't for the constant interruptions every time we watch an episode.

Watching these two shows taking place in two cities where tiles are abundant, Patrick will rewind and pause to either criticize, observe, or approve every single tiling job. Whether in bathrooms, bathtubs (my Lord, so many bathtubs in *Dexter*!), kitchens, or kitchen counters. Plus, the occasional embalming lab or morgue.

"Oh man," he will say, shaking his head and keeping his eyes riveted on the offensive shower tile, oblivious to the beautiful half-naked woman inches away (the one on TV, not me). "Look at how thick this grout is, Marina!"

In addition to interrupting the show right before the most thrilling part – the discovery of a body in the bathtub or the passionate sex in the shower – he has to involve me in his critiques.

- "Marina! Look! Look and tell me what's wrong with this picture?"

- "The colors?" I offer timidly.

- "No! Look! They picked a 6-inch bullnose to match the 4x4 tiles!" (I learned a few technical terms during my confinement)

- "Ugh!!! You're right!!!" (I try to look as shocked and disgusted as I can.)

As I should. I once seemed ambivalent and he immediately pulled a pencil out of his pocket and demonstrated on a sheet of paper the unharmonious result caused by poor alignment. Let's not get into its disastrous consequences on a tile floor grouting.

That absentmindedness of mine cost me 15 minutes of the show.

I'm already thinking I need to find a series taking place in the 70's, when most tubs were made of molded plastic and floors were carpeted wall-to-wall!

Le Petit tips on lettuce and crudités:

Soft radishes? Revive them by soaking them for a few hours in a large amount of cold water and vinegar. They'll be crunchy again. You can do this to pretty much all crudités.

If your lettuce starts to wilt, before you add it to your compost try soaking it in sweetened water for one hour; it will get its crunchiness back.

Did you put too much vinegar into your salad? Again? Add a small ball of white bread to it and toss it around. It will absorb the excess of vinegar.

CHAPTER 4
Desserts

I often make a few alterations to recipes I borrow from others.

I always melt my chocolate in a bowl over steam, never directly on the burner. The bowl should not touch the water; the steam is what melts the chocolate.

If the recipe calls for just butter or just oil, I prefer a blend of equal amounts of butter and oil. The oil gives it a moistness you would not get with just butter unless you keep your cake out for a while before you serve it. The butter gives that delicious taste you want in a cake.

As far as my choice of oil goes, I like to bake with peanut oil which is very light. One cake here involves olive oil. Olive oil is delicious, but it will definitely transfer its taste to your cake. This does not go very well with many cakes; it is mostly for the most exotic ones, prepared with spices or herbs.

And finally, I systematically only use 2/3 to 3/4 of the amount of sugar mentioned in the recipe. It is a safe bet, unless you are preparing a meringue, *bien sûr*, in which case the amount of sugar must be respected. Or a cake like a *Génoise,* which involves a small amount of flour and gets its consistency from the other ingredients.

As far as proceedings go, I usually follow the same order, even if the recipe tells you to mix all the ingredients at once. I do not care for the mixing-all-ingredients-at-once method. First, I mix my oil and butter. The butter must be soft enough to mix easily with the oil. I then add the sugar and mix well until creamy. The eggs come next, one at a time.

Then I add the flour, which I will have mixed with the sifted salt and baking powder and/or soda. I am rather indifferent when it comes to sifting flour – I find that a good energetic whisk will aerate it and eliminate the lumps just as well. But the salt, soda and baking powder, I always sift.

If the recipe calls for milk (or any dairy product), I add the flour mixture and the milk alternatively, no more than one-third at a time, and I mix until smooth after each addition.

If the cake involves beaten egg whites, those are added at the end, *bien sûr.*

I sometimes add boiling water to the batter quickly, right before I put the cake in the oven (thus have your pan buttered before you do that). A tip passed on to me by my friend, Matt, who has introduced me to many delicious desserts from the southern states. It gives your cake an interesting moist character. Naturally, do not add boiling water if you prepare a cake with beaten egg whites or a cake involving very little flour, such as a *Génoise*. It's just for cakes which are supposed to be moist and doughy. Like most American cakes.

The ratio would be 1 cup of boiling water for 2 (or slightly more) cups of flour. And if you do so, slightly underbake your cake. When you insert your toothpick (or whatever you choose to insert), a few crumbs should still cling to it.

The boiling water thing is definitely not French. But keep in mind, Yours Truly is now more on the Hoosier side than the French one. I'm a *Froosier*, as my friend, Cordah, calls me.

If the recipe calls for milk, I prefer using a richer milk such as evaporated or coconut. A very slight flavor of coconut will linger if you use coconut milk, but that goes with most cakes. I am not a big fan of buttermilk.

Last, but not least, even if not specified, always add a good pinch of salt.

A perfect cake is often a collective affair made of many contributions from your friends.

When I first came to the States, many dishes I had seen in my *Topolino* magazine (the Italian version of Mickey Mouse) years earlier that had always intrigued me very much suddenly made sense.

When very young, I was a staunch reader of *Topolino,* but I could not begin to understand most of the food, particularly a certain dish with a crust on top. The only dishes with crusts on top I knew were savory and certainly not eaten with ice cream! When asked, my family could only provide very vague answers such as, "I don't know, these stories take place in America. God only knows what they eat!"

And that marvelous three-layer cake with chocolate sauce dripping down its sides? I had never seen such a cake in pastry shops before! I remember asking Nonna, my grandmother, if she could make one, but after a brief inspection of the picture she went back to whatever she was cooking and probably told me she'd do it later when she had the time.

Do not feel sorry for me, though; I ate plenty of delicious cakes while growing up, but I had to wait more than 10 years before I could finally eat a pie like the ones in *Topolino.* And I finally understood what it was: an apple pie à la mode!

Me, trying to understand American desserts.

Marina Cake

It is the name a young boy gave to the cake I prepared for his family. When asked what he wanted for his birthday, he answered, "I want Marina Cake."

This one is for you, Gus.

For 12 to 16 people:

- 4 oz. of unsweetened chocolate.
- 1½ c. of sugar
- ¾ c. of butter and oil. And by that, I mean ¾ c. of both combined. I will do the math for you: 3/4 stick of butter (room temp) and a little less than 1/3 c. of oil. Don't worry too much about the measurement. It's not a chemistry project, nothing's going to explode.
- 3 large eggs
- 2 c. flour
- 1½ tsp. baking powder
- 1 tsp. baking soda
- 1 tsp. salt
- A little vanilla
- 1½ c. coconut milk (one can) or evaporated milk. Or buttermilk, if you must.
- 1 c. boiling water.

Preheat your oven to 350°F. Butter and flour your cake mold.

Melt your chocolate over steam.

Sift together flour, baking soda, baking powder and salt. I told you how I sift, choose the method you prefer.

Mix your butter and oil, add sugar, and mix well. Add the eggs one at a time and keep mixing until the mixture feels a little lighter and looks a little paler. This is the way most cakes get started.

Start adding your flour mixture, a large spoonful at a time, while you alternate it with the milk.

Now you can add the chocolate and vanilla and, at the very last second just before you put your cake in the oven, throw in the boiling water. Stir gently but as quickly as possible.

Bake for about 50 minutes.

If you want to prepare a two-layer cake, then bake the two thinner cakes for just 30 minutes.

This recipe is perfect for all sorts of cakes; you just need to adapt the icing: Pecans and coconut for German Chocolate, cherries and cream for Black Forest, etc.…

If you want a mocha cake, just throw in a few teaspoons of instant coffee with your chocolate instead of vanilla – I'd say two or three. This could be served with a coffee cream cheese icing, which is much simpler to prepare than a real buttercream. By real, I mean the one which involves syrup. Besides, a coffee cream cheese icing is more in the character of this particular mocha cake, which has a simpler, more artisanal flavor than most of the French cakes involving buttercream.

More About Icings

While we are on the subject of icings, I will tell you how I prepare mine, which has always been enjoyed and holds for a long time on wedding cakes, usually waiting on a table for quite some time. Although, I do remember a certain wedding cake which waited for a long time outside on a hot summer day, and on a table placed on a slight slope, which did not hold that well…

1/3 of the weight of the cream cheese in butter. For example, 2/3 stick of butter for 8 oz. of cream-cheese. (My amount of butter is off by 3 grams. Not bad.)

1 c. confectioner's sugar

The flavor of your choice. I suggest vanilla for a wedding cake, but it can be coffee, instant or a few tbsps. of strong espresso. Or roasted coconut for a coconut cake.

Mix your cream cheese and your soft butter together. Add your sifted sugar and your flavor. Now, note that although I am not a sifter, I always sift confectioner's sugar.

About my Mother

Mom did not exactly teach me how to cook and I never asked her to. Now I wish I had asked her to show me how to prepare some of her dishes, or how to sew, instead of wasting my time in cafés.

But I had a great advantage: I knew how the final product was supposed to taste even if I had never prepared it before. Having references plays an important part in cooking.

She was an excellent cook and eating her food for so many years before being on my own guided me when, for instance, I had to judge the saltiness of a stew or correct the thickness of a sauce. Knowing what you are aiming for is a great advantage.

In short, she trained my palate.

Besides, I was only using French or Italian books in which directions are very vague when it comes to certain ingredients and seasonings in particular. "Salt and a little pepper," "a nice piece," and "a handful" was all you got. A well-adjusted palate and common sense are important.

But she was always willing to share her knowledge. If I seemed interested in what she was doing, or was just lingering in the kitchen a bit longer than usual, she'd say something like, "If you have time, I can show you now how to prepare a Béchamel. I need some for my Pasta al Forno." And while making the sauce she would inform me she always added some to her Lasagna, too. And so do I.

She also randomly sowed little bits of information while she was working. "The next time you make crêpes, spread the butter with a slice of potato; no need to burn a good brush." Or, "If you ever put too much salt in a soup, throw in a peeled potato! You'll be surprised to see how much salt a potato can absorb."

For many years I learned all sorts of tips which often saved the show later.

Mom was horrified the first time she came to visit and saw me throwing away the vegetables I used to make the broth for a sauce. "Strain them and blend them into your sauce," she said. "They lost their flavor but will add a bit more substance to it!" My generation's mothers (tomorrow is Mothers' Day!) were a lot like her: nothing went to waste. A habit I have kept.

Patrick takes the zero-waste thing to a whole new level: all liquids are saved for the plants (they do not seem to mind the cocktail water/cream/coke/wine), the coffee grounds go to trees and plants, and any food waste to feed a friend's chickens or compost. I often joke with new employees that Patrick's training is more about trees and plants than about customers.

Patrick's priorities.

When I came here, I discovered a whole new world of techniques I had never suspected existed. Mixing all ingredients at once? Pressing a crust with fingers? But before I taught myself how to cook and put some of these techniques to work, I – like many immigrants at the time – was very much seduced by the products I discovered in supermarkets designed to simplify the life of the cook of the house.

Such as boxed cakes.

I could not believe it! Everything was in that box except for the eggs and some water. A dream come true! I remember my roommates at the time being very intrigued by this woman, coming from the Land of Good Cooks, in awe of boxed cakes or ecstatic while eating a Ding-Dong. A boxed cake of some sort was part of our everyday diet during my first semester here.

And by the end of my fifth month here I had gained 10 lbs. (Contrary to popular belief, French women do get fat).

The first time I went back to France, mom took one look at me and suggested I bring back a couple of her cookbooks to the States. It is then I realized it was time to start preparing our meals, and that's how I discovered the pleasure of preparing tarte aux pommes or a Clafoutis.

Every first time French cook's dream: boxed cakes and Ding-Dongs.

Me, some fifteen years later discovering
American desserts!

Mon Gâteau aux Myrtilles/My Blueberry Cake

When my daughter, Anna-Caterina, asked me for the recipe of my blueberry cake, I was first annoyed by her request. I hadn't made this cake in a long time and I never write my recipes down. It's all in my head and my head should be the last place to be trusted with my recipes because my memory is poor. But for some reason I keep trusting it...

Prepare a *Quatre-quarts* (recipe in a few pages) and spread the batter in a mold high enough to accommodate twice its height (do not beat the egg whites). Add a pound of fresh blueberries on top and spread a layer of cream you prepare with 1 c. sour cream, ¼ c. sugar, 1 egg yolk and a bit of vanilla.

Like for most cakes, you will need to preheat your oven to 350°F, but this one will take almost twice as long to bake; the weight of fruit and cream will prevent it from rising as fast. Check it after 45 minutes or so.

Am I going to be responsible for every failure my readers encounter while preparing one of my recipes? Keep in mind this is NOT a cookbook, as I made it clear on page one. And it is my first one, too!

Actually, it isn't. My wedding present to a lovely young woman, Brynnen, was a small cookbook (a real cookbook!) of most of the recipes she and her family enjoyed over the years.

Fondant au Chocolat/Flourless Chocolate Cake

As simple as a mousse. The French serve it as a cake, but it can be a tart, baked in a shell made with rice flour and nuts. I prefer the latter, which is easier to serve. No need to prebake the crust since this cake needs to bake at least a couple of hours.

- 10 oz. of semi-sweet chocolate
- 5 to 6 oz. of butter
- 1 c. sugar
- 8 large eggs, separated.
- 2 good tbsps. of brandy, rum or instant coffee if you do not want the alcohol (although this cake bakes for at least 2 hours and the alcohol will be long gone)

Preheat your oven at a very low temperature, 250°F.

Melt your chocolate, butter, and alcohol in a bowl over simmering water. When melted, add your sugar and let it melt a little too, stirring once in a while.

When the chocolate mixture looks smooth enough, remove the bowl from the stove and add the yolks while whisking vigorously. Beat your egg whites until fluffy and add them to your preparation, which at this point will be a bit cooler.

Pour the batter into your buttered mold, or crust, and let cook for a good 2 hours. If you forget it for an extra 30 minutes, it's just fine.

If you choose to bake it into a crust, prepare a sweet one with 1 c. of flour (or rice flour which is gluten-free), 6 oz. of butter, a couple of tbsps. of sugar and a ½ c. of the chopped nuts of your choice. You can add 1 tbsp. of cocoa powder, too. And a pinch of salt, never forget the salt in your crusts even in sweet ones.

Mix all ingredients with fingers (if you use a food processor add the nuts later, no need to pulverize them). Add enough water so that you can press it into your mold, and a little more if you prefer rolling it.

I have a confession. Once in a while, I enjoy torturing people who exercise on the B-Line, the trail that cuts through town and runs by my kitchen window. Isn't it horrible? I enjoy tormenting them, tantalizing them with the deliciously tempting fragrance of chocolate, vanilla, and hazelnuts pouring out of my window.

I swear I do not want to sabotage their efforts, though. No, I want people to be healthy and do the right thing; it is just that it gives me great pleasure to observe a quivering nostril, a melancholy gaze toward my window, a nose trying to capture that wonderful scent.

I do apologize if you happen to be one of my victims. You do not need to plot revenge though; it has already been done.

Some time ago I noticed with great pleasure an entire class working out on the B-Line and soon realized it met every week! What an opportunity, surely, not to be wasted. I started staging Machiavellian baking sessions involving the most delicious scents one can imagine and it worked for a couple weeks. The students seemed to be distracted, slightly slowing down their pace when passing by the window, venturing a timid and guilty gaze towards me. I was in heaven. Not for long.

On the third week, I went all out: peaches and chocolate! When I saw the class running towards me, I approached the window, pretending to be busy reorganizing the pots on the ledge. To my great dismay, I did not notice ONE SINGLE REACTION! What happened?!? Not a single person in the group reacted to the perfume of peaches from Georgia and Belgian chocolate?!? Surely, it had to be a mistake!

So, on the following week I stepped up: chocolate with Grand Marnier! Well, that will teach them for ignoring me!

NOTHING AGAIN! Not one nostril moved, not one gaze became dreamy, no legs slowed down. As if I did not exist!

I then realized, first with anger but soon with great sadness, I was the victim of a mutiny! I imagined their meeting in the locker room: "Pretend you do not smell anything special," ordered the teacher. "Do not let her see one muscle move! Remain focused, look straight ahead!" And then with an ugly smile, "We will show her!"

Me, by the Window circa 2020 and 2017.

A musing on herbs, before the rosemary cake with sage custard.

If only herbs could talk. That's what I was wondering while preparing my sage custard. Did you notice some herbs cannot do anything alone and some can't stand one another's company?

Having been raised in France, my favorite herb is Tarragon. So sweet, so delicate; I have never had the heart to tell her she would not have been as successful without Shallot's help.

But also being Italian, I am deeply in love with Basil, too. Basil, however, is anything but timid. His arrogance gets a bit on my nerves at times and more than once I have reminded him he had no reason to be so cocky. *Pfff!* he usually replies with a shrug.

On the other hand, Thyme and Laurel feel no qualms about admitting they need one another. I could be wrong, and although I know Laurel is stronger, I also suspect he is a bit more dependent. Not that I would ever mention it to him.

Sage and Rosemary have wonderful dispositions. They do very well in a group, as well on their own. Quite self-sufficient, they are also very accommodating and gracious toward others. That is the sort of humble mind I respect, none of that I-need-no-one attitude.

And Parsley, of course! He is our loyal friend; always around and willing to help, whatever we need. We sometimes tend to take him for granted, too. How many times have I forgotten to give him the regal seat he deserves on my plates?

But let's go back to the rosemary cake and my sage custard. I prepare all sorts of custards, from saffron or cardamom to caramelized garlic. I call them mine because I like to think I thought of them first. And maybe I did.

Olive Oil Cake with Rosemary and Sage Custard

This is a *Génoise* made with olive oil. *Génoise* being a sponge cake to which some rosemary is added. I try the best I can to remember where I have read this or that or which of my friends gave me such idea but it's not always possible to credit people after so many years. I do not keep recipes nicely organized in a box – it's all in my head – and besides, recipes travel and constantly get slightly modified. It happens that I sometimes assume I was the first to think of something genius, to later realize 20 chefs have already thought of it. Darn Googling!

This recipe involves many ingredients; therefore I will divide them into groups:

1. ¾ c. flour, sifted (the way you prefer, the old way or my way) with ¾ tsp. of baking powder and ½ tsp. of salt
2. 2 eggs, ½ c. sugar mixed with 1 tbsp. of crushed rosemary. Fresh, so important!
3. 1/3 c. of olive oil (oil only, no butter), 2 tsps. lemon juice
4. 3 tbsps. melted butter

In a bowl over gently simmering water, (again, bowl should not touch the water) mix #2 just a few minutes until it gets warm.

Remove the bowl as soon as you can feel the warmth on your clean finger (sorry, but I am writing this in times of Coronavirus and one can't be too careful). If you let it get too hot, your cake will be dry.

Using an electric blender, whisk your eggs/sugar at high speed until their volume doubles. You can do it by hand, but it will take much longer.

Add #3, and just give it a quick whisk.

Add #1 by hand, and as delicately and quickly as you can.

Finally, drizzle in your butter and give it a quick final mix.

Bake at 350°F for 50-60 minutes.

I always serve this cake with sage custard, a *Crème Anglaise* to which I add a couple of sage leaves.

Boil 1 pint of milk. While your milk warms up, whisk vigorously (by hand or in a blender) 6 yolks with ½ c. of sugar until it looks smooth and a bit paler.

When the milk is ready, lower your heat to a minimum and add, always whisking, your eggs/ sugar. Keep on stirring, now with a wooden spoon, until your mixture "coats the spoon," which simply means that if you draw a line on the back of the spoon with your, again, clean finger, the line will stay.

Remove immediately from the stove, so it will not keep on cooking on the warm burner, and now you can add a few leaves of sage. Fresh, needless to say. Let it cool before serving.

Later I will mention *Crème Anglaise* should be served with the *Marquise au Chocolat*. This would be the recipe to follow, minus the sage.

Quatre-Quarts

Americans eat Pound Cake, the French, *Quatre-Quarts*. Pretty much the same thing: same weight – not volume – of flour, sugar, eggs and butter.

For a small cake for 8:

1 c. flour, 2/3 c. sugar, 3 small eggs, 10 tbsps. butter. In this cake I only use butter. And of course, 1 tsp. of baking powder and the obligatory pinch of salt if you use unsalted butter, which I always do.

Do the usual thing. Mix soft butter with sugar, add eggs one at a time, your flour already sifted with salt and powder. Bake at 350°F for about 30 minutes.

The original recipe for *Quatre-Quarts* says to separate the eggs and add the beaten whites at the end. But you know, I often don't bother.

You can add pretty much what you want to the batter: dry fruit, nuts, fresh fruit which doesn't take long to cook, or even fruit sauces. If you make it with a fruit sauce, such as apple or bananas, for instance, then it becomes (in my Not-a-Cookbook) a Five-Fifths. After the flour you add an equal weight of fruit.

> Le Petit tip:
>
> To prevent your nuts, dried fruit, or chocolate chips from falling at the bottom of your cake, shake them in a bit of flour before you add them to the batter. The fine coat of flour will keep them in place.

How is it possible to write a cookbook and not share some memories? I've got a head full of memories, more memories than recipes. They keep me company when I work alone or cannot sleep at night. Memories of customers we fed when they were young and whose children we feed now.

Memories of weddings or rehearsal dinners, birthdays and anniversaries, and sadly, memorials too. It is impossible to write a recipe and not remember who was so fond of it.

Memories of customers and employees, too. I have no idea how many people we have employed over the years. 200? Some only stayed one year or two but most have stayed for the duration of their studies or their time in the restaurant business or in Bloomington. And one of their friends or a sibling takes over when they leave. In Hans' case, he and his two brothers successively worked here! We have employed children of former employees and of customers too, of course. Isn't it something?

Crème Caramel

Nothing is easier to prepare than a *Crème Caramel*.

- 1 liter of milk (a little teensy more than a quart)
- 12 medium eggs, of which you only keep 4 whites. Keep the other 8 whites for a Dacquoise (I would give you the recipe but since I am using Jacques Pépin's you might as well buy that book, too) or a white cake.
- 1 c. sugar, vanilla.

First, prepare your caramel:

Put 3/4 c. sugar, 2 tbsps. water and 3 drops of lemon juice in a small pot. Place the pot on the burner, not too high if you're also doing something else, but I do not encourage multitasking when preparing a caramel!

Let it cook until the color gets to a nice golden brown.

Pour it in your mold while you rotate the mold to spread the caramel all over its sides. If you have a fan, turn it on; a burnt caramel will smoke your entire house.

If you happen to be a customer (I'm hoping a few of you are reading this, this project was originally meant just for you, you know?) you may have noticed I prefer dark caramels, on the edge of being burnt. I find the slightly bitter taste counterbalances very nicely the sweetness of such desserts. The caramel can now wait forever.

Drawing of Anna burning the Caramel
(which, of course, never happened)

Bring the milk and vanilla to a boil. Meanwhile, mix well your sugar with the 4 whole eggs and the 8 yolks.

When the milk is ready, add it slowly to the egg mixture while whisking and pour the whole thing in your mold.

Place in a *bain-marie* (double bath, meaning you place the mold into a larger one filled ½ way with water) and bake for about 40 minutes in a medium/hot oven, at 400°F.

When the crème looks set, check the inside with a knife as you would if you baked a cake; it should come out dry.

Let it cool off in the fridge before you attempt to unmold it. Even prepare it the day before you intend to serve it.

The little bubbles you will see on the sides of your crème are the sign of a perfect Crème Caramel.

Bravo!

If not, do not give up; it's a delicious dessert.

Next time try it with pistachios – it is my favorite. Add a good handful of chopped nuts to your milk while it is warming up on a slightly lower burner. Stir once in a while to make sure the nuts are not burning at the bottom of your pot.

My Mousse au Chocolat

I call it mine because it is a bit richer than most mousses: it calls for more butter. It's a dessert between a *Mousse* and a *Marquise*. The latter would use more butter, be frozen and served with *Crème Anglaise*.

For 8 people:

- 9 oz. of semi-sweet chocolate
- 8 large eggs
- Cream of tartar, or a pinch of salt with a few drops of lemon juice to whip the egg whites
- 2/3 stick of unsalted butter
- A couple tbsps. of something strong and delicious, such as Rum or Brandy.

In a bowl over steam, melt your chocolate with your liquor. Keep in mind whenever you melt chocolate over steam that the bowl should not touch the water. The steam melts the chocolate, not the water. Stir occasionally.

While it melts, separate your eggs.

When your chocolate has melted, add the butter cut in small pieces and blend well. When all the butter has been added, stir your egg yolks into the bowl. This can be done by hand or with a mixer.

When your chocolate/butter/yolks mixture looks smooth, set it aside and let it cool off a little.

Now that your mixture has cooled off a bit (it can still be slightly warm), whip your egg whites until stiff with whichever option you prefer – most French people just use a pinch of salt, or salt with a few drops of lemon juice. Americans tend to prefer cream of tartar. You are now ready to fold the whites into the chocolate mixture.

This step has to be done fast but gently, by hand with a wooden spoon. A little at a time, not all at once. You must add the whites to the chocolate, not the other way around. A heavier weight on beaten egg whites would deflate them.

You fold 1/3 of the whites gently into the chocolate. Add the second third, mix carefully, and finally the rest of the whites. Your mousse is ready to be refrigerated and can wait for a couple of days.

Le Petit tips:

In order to get stiffer egg whites or whipped cream, start beating at a low speed and then increase to a maximal one when it starts to foam.

When you whip cream, put your whisk and bowl in the freezer for 10 minutes. It will whip faster and the cream will be lighter.

Drawing of me whipping egg whites

Panna Cotta

Super simple. I know I say that a lot, but *Panna Cotta* is truly super simple.

- 1¼ c. of cream (again, when I mention cream, I always mean whipping cream)
- 1 tsp. gelatin
- 1 or 2 tbsps. brown sugar. No more.

Heat the cream and sugar on a medium heat. Bring it to the verge of boiling, stirring once in a while, but do not let it boil; an unaesthetic skin will form on top of your cream while cooling.

Meanwhile, mix your gelatin in a little bit of cold water and whisk it into the cream when the cream is cooked. That's what *Panna Cotta* means in Italian: cooked cream.

Pour it into individual ramequins or a large crown-shaped mold. Put it in your fridge and let it cool.

If you choose a large mold, just dip it in very hot water for a few seconds and flip it over a plate; the *Panna Cotta* will come right out of it.

It is traditionally served with fruit or a fruit sauce, but if you prefer, you can mix in 1 tsp. of instant coffee before refrigerating it.

Tarte Tatin

Tarte Tatin will always be one of my favorite desserts and it keeps very well in the fridge for a few days. You can also prepare it with other fruit, as long as they're not too juicy. Pumpkins make wonderful Tatin, as my friend Anita prepared for me. I sometimes prepare it with shallots, which makes a delicious appetizer.

But this is the original recipe, with apples. The one the Tatin sisters created by accident, as it sometimes happens. They dropped the pie upside down and realized it looked more appetizing that way.

Prepare a short crust pastry (*pâte brisée*) with 1 c. of flour and ¾ stick of butter, salt, and a few tbsps. of water until a ball forms. No more. *Pâte brisée* is the unsweetened crust you prepare for quiches. I suggest water but it can be ½ egg with a little milk as Jacques Pépin suggests in one of his books (I love that man. Did you read *The Apprentice*? If you haven't yet, you must).

By the way, I never use salted butter, but if you do, skip the obligatory pinch of salt I always mention.

Roll it as thin as you can on a piece of wax paper and put it aside while you prepare the apples. Peel and slice your apples, not too thin (a couple of pounds should do for a small pie).

Tartes Tatin

Prepare a caramel with ½ c. of sugar and do not let it get too dark for it will cook more in the oven. (same caramel recipe as *Crème Caramel*); pour it in your pie mold.

Place your slices of apples on your caramel, creating a nice pattern. Make sure the slices have their round side down so that when you unmold the tart it will look prettier. Cut a few small pieces of unsalted butter on your apples and do not be afraid to use too much! I would say no less than 2 oz.

Flip your waxed paper on top, detach it from the dough, prick the dough with a fork and bake at 350°F for about 30 minutes.

Flip the tarte on your serving plate while it's still hot, otherwise the apples will stick to the caramel when it cools. And choose a large serving plate for there may be quite a bit of juice that comes out.

You know, most recipes will tell you to sprinkle sugar on the mold instead of preparing a caramel. I personally find the caramelized look more appetizing. And since I use a caramel, I skip adding more sugar on the fruit. Less sugar, more butter. That is my motto, which you may have already guessed (or already know if you are a customer).

If you prepare a savory Tatin though, use very little caramel.

Tiramisù

This is the traditional recipe – THE original recipe from Piedmont – the only one my 100% Piedmontese mother would consider.

As you have noticed by now, I am all for adapting recipes to one's taste and making a few minor alterations to them. When it comes to *Tiramisù*, though, no substitutions for ladyfingers or Mascarpone. Even the alcohol is important. Without it, sure, it will be delicious, but it will lack that little kick. That part of its name – *sù* – meaning *up*!

If you are looking for an Italian cookbook, I suggest Claudia Roden's. The recipes are authentic, very well explained and organized by region. Suffice to say, my mother's recipe differs very little from hers:

- Ladyfinger cookies, about two dozen
- 1/2 c. of espresso (or very strong coffee), rum (about 4 to 6 tbsps.; up to you but it should not cover the taste of coffee) plus a little brandy or Cognac, half the amount of rum
- 1 lb. mascarpone, 2 eggs (separated), 5 or 6 tbsps. confectioner's sugar and enough unsweetened cocoa powder to cover the top of your cake

Mix the cheese with the egg yolks and the sugar, and add the whites beaten stiff but not dry.

Dip the cookies into the liquids you will have mixed together. Let them soak up the good stuff but you don't want them to get too soft. Place them in a glass mold.

Spread the mascarpone cream on your cookies. I noticed Claudia does only one layer of cookies; Mom preferred two layers, alternating the cookies and mascarpone. Whether you choose one or two layers, cover the final layer of cream with a generous layer of well-sifted cocoa.

It will be enough for 6 to 8 people and you can prepare it the day before.

CHAPTER 5
Windows and Family

And now, all about my Saturday morning Window, which I have operated during the farmers' market for the last 12 seasons.

I love all my Windows. The first ones, when I only offered a crêpe, a dessert, and regular coffee. The cold and slow ones; the warm and busy ones. The ones I take inside when it's too cold. And even the socially distanced ones. But most of all, I love our customers, who have supported it through heat waves, torrential rains and viruses. They have amazed me during these difficult times of Corona.

I wish I could name you all, but you know how expensive printing is. Besides, you know I am thinking of you.

Thank you.

My Window along the years

Food prepping with Anna in the morning

One of my favorite food memories are the meals Anna and I shared while I was convalescing after a surgery. She decided she would cook dinner for me every night for a week. "You will starve if I don't cook for you!" she said.

She was only 12 and took the job very seriously. On the weekend before her week in the kitchen, she studied a little book she had won at her school and selected seven different pasta recipes. She loved her pasta.

She made a list of all she needed and sent her dad shopping. Every day upon returning from school she asked me which recipe I would prefer and started cooking. I have fond memories of those seven meals we shared, me in bed and Anna sitting next to me. She was so proud and happy I never had the heart to tell her that pasta was probably not what I should eat after my surgery. At least, not every day during the first week. Besides, it was so delicious!

Anna and me

In this book, I mention my daughter more often than my son for the simple reason that Anna was more involved in the preparation of the food. Winston was especially involved in eating it.

While writing the recipe for my mayonnaise, I was reminded of the mango mayonnaise I had prepared for him and Rachel for one of their visits to Bloomington about two years ago, during which I broke my ankle. My first brush with confinement and it was a long one: three months!

This episode of my life would have turned into a bad memory had it not been for the fantastic job our employees and Patrick did at the Window and Sunday brunch, the only two shifts the restaurant maintained.

One those Sunday brunches, as fate would have it, turned out to be one of the busiest ones ever, and Patrick nearly lost his mind. But our regulars did not complain because that's how they are: understanding and supportive. As a matter of fact, our friends Jill and Jace still talk about the amazing mashed potatoes Patrick had to improvise. I tried to duplicate them, but to no avail.

Besides, all the delicious food and treats and beautiful flowers and plants and cards our customers brought me turned a potentially sad and boring summer into a rather pleasant one. Thinking about it, I almost wish I would break the other ankle...

The summer of the broken ankle!

We all think of Bloomington as a very safe place, but 20 years ago it was so safe we would not even think of locking our car at night and we live downtown! Patrick took his trust in Bloomington a bit further: he even left the keys in the ignition.

During one of my parents' visits, my dad remarked it was not very prudent to leave the keys in the car at night and I can still hear myself laughing: "Oh, Dad! We are not in Paris! We do not have to worry about such things here!"

Well, my friends, as fate would have it, our car was stolen on that very night! I was devastated: not only my favorite Renault was gone but I would look like a complete idiot! So, being the liar I can be at desperate times, when my dad asked me where the car was, I answered that we had to take it to the garage, but that it did not seem to be very bad (whatever I said it was…).

After a few days, Dad suggested he should look at the car since he did not have much to do. I had to come up with another excuse.

A day or two later, the sheriff informed us our car had been found in Linton, further west. Just a joy ride; one of my tapes and a basketball were missing.

Although my dad never saw the sheriff, I still told him the truth because, quite frankly, at that point the story was too funny not to be shared! My mother laughed and my dad just rolled his eyes.

It happened again 17 years later.

Like I said, the first time I was devastated; I loved my Renault Encore but when it was stolen again after almost two decades of being driven by yours truly and a husband who turns all cars into recycling bins, I was relieved to hear it had disappeared. Seeing that piece of junk sitting in front of the restaurant made my heart sink.

Some of you might remember the theft of our car; an article was published in the auto section of *The Herald Times*, our local paper. For a long time, customers inquired about the stolen Renault after reading the article I framed and placed in the men's bathroom (I believe Laura Lane, the reporter, wasn't too impressed by my choice of placement, but a captive audience always works if you need attention).

So, when Patrick informed me the car had been stolen, I felt a pang of joy. But, being a sympathetic wife, I managed to utter a forced, "Oh…I am so sorry."

That's when I first tried to conceive some diabolical plan to let people know a red Peugeot – in even worse shape – would be waiting with the keys under the seat, along with an invitation for two dinners.

Still waiting, by the way.

In this book, as I said earlier, I barely mention our son, Winston, and I feel I should remedy this injustice.

I could fill pages and pages about Winston, for he always had his own rather original agenda, but I will limit myself to sharing the 4 most important things he's done so far:

1. In 2011, fresh out of the U.S. Marine Corps, he used the money he made deployed in Afghanistan to embark on a great mission: a 5,000-mile trek through Southeast Asia to raise money for cleft palate facial reconstructive surgeries for children. He did it to help Dr. Williams' foundation, ICSF. Dr. Jeffrey Williams performed the surgeries mostly throughout Southeast Asia and South America – and probably still does – only charging around $250 to cover the price of supplies. It always makes us proud and happy to think of those 300 children confidently smiling thanks to the money Winston raised.
2. In 2015, he married Rachel.
3. In 2019, Felix was born.
4. And at the end of that same year, he and Rachel started building their home in New Orleans, which will also double as a short-term rental on Airbnb.

Not the best time to start in the tourism industry, but who could predict such a pandemic? But, this book started as a confinement project to take my mind off of Coronavirus (Corona the Mean Virus, as I call it in my book for Felix) and I do not want to end it on a sad note. Thus, I will share a few more stories with you.

Winston, Rachel, Felix and their home in New Orleans

The next two stories are about my very ecologically driven husband.

My husband walking around holding a piece of beef fat in one hand and a leather boot in the other is a familiar sight. Beef fat is a very good leather conditioner indeed, and we have access to a free and inexhaustible source.

Beef fat is a rite of passage for Le Petit Café's employees. All of them, sooner or later, must accept to have their winter boots rubbed with beef fat.

Some have loved it and may even have continued to do so. Some still resist the idea and others have complained they were followed home by stray dogs and cats.

The most adamantly averse to it (like me) have simply switched to suede or rubber boots.

Employee followed home by stray animals

A customer once told me she saw Patrick picking up trash in a supermarket parking lot. Yes. I told her that whenever he visits a store, he does that and saves it for the recycling center or our shredder. what she does not know is that he continues to do so even when we leave town or even the country!

For instance, he always brings back to Bloomington small juice bottles from various airports ("I must, Marina; I have read many airports do not recycle," or "I do not trust this airport").

When we travel in the States it is not so bad but when we go abroad the trash *definitely* gets in the way of souvenirs, especially in developing countries. Of course, Patrick understands that some countries have more urgent issues to address before they can spend money on recycling, but he also feels he has to do his part to help.

Here is, verbatim, the conversation we had before our return from Peru:

- "We have bought enough souvenirs, Marina. We are running out of room."
- "We still have a little space in the suitcase."
- "I need the paper for our shredder."
- "But you always use your traveling bag for that!"
- "It's already filled with plastic bottles."

To the collection of recyclable goods we must add the various edible items saved from the flights. My Lord – I hate it when we have to fly in more than two planes!

Thank God for the food restrictions on domestic airlines. You will never hear ME complain about the missing peanuts! As exciting as they are, international flights are trying. We always arrived at my parents' house with our bags filled with yogurts, fruit salads, cheddar cheese and cookies, and Patrick always insisted on saving the muffins and bread for the kids (or the pigeons...or an occasional duck).

- "You know Winston, Marina! He will be hungry later."
- "But there is plenty to eat at my parents'!"
- "There is always a wait at the rental car booth."

What killed me, though, is that whenever we came back from France, the Air France butter cookies that he brought back for the kids had as much success as my souvenirs.

At the beginning of confinement, I shared on Facebook that I was writing a cookbook. A very artisanal book, I said. No glossy pages and professional binding. Not even a cookbook, a book like the one you just read, a potpourri of memories, recipes, and a few tips. And two complaints.

I was contemplating with a certain lack of enthusiasm what such an artisanal project entailed. Ordering more paper, making sure my printer had enough ink (color, too?). Perforating all those pages (thank God Patrick just located a three-hole puncher in his cave, that will save time!). Buying cheap folders because paying to have them bound would be too costly – but how many? Etc., etc. Then, a few weeks ago I got a very kind offer from Michael, a customer of ours who works at AuthorHouse: a free starter package.

In a few seconds I went from:

> *Where am I going to find some free stickers? The post office used to leave some in the lobby, I wonder if they still do…But wait, many people know me at the post office! I'll never hear the end of it…And my friend Bill works there, too! He's going to retire soon though, but still…I will cut off Priority Mail, separate them in three vertical sections and stick them on the spine. No one will recognize them.*

to:

> *My book online and maybe on bookstore shelves?!?*

Maybe this project wouldn't be such a headache, after all, I told myself. It suddenly felt like my artisanal project might actually become a reality. And now, here we are.

So, to all of you – whether you bought this book in a bookstore or online – I hope you enjoyed reading it as much as I enjoyed writing it.

With love,

Marina

Acknowledgements

I thank Michael for making publishing this book possible.

Anna-Caterina for spending the holidays editing it.

Maureen for helping me organize the photos and drawings.

Carmen for encouraging me and suggesting "Not a Cookbook" would make a great title.

Patrick for being a good sport about being teased.

And, of course, thank you to all of our customers and employees over the years. Without you, I wouldn't have nearly as many wonderful memories to share.

Printed in the United States
By Bookmasters